STARTER VEGETABLE GARDENS:

A Practical Guide to
Grow Your Vegetables and Fruit.
Discover the Effectiveness of Growing Your Garden by Using the Raised Bed Technique.
Grow More Using Less Space!

By: ***Aida Campbell***

TABLE OF CONTENTS

Introduction

The key to successful raised garden beds is planning out your garden. This need not be stressful but does require taking a little time to assess a variety of considerations. It is well worth sketching out your garden to determine the best location and size of beds. Ideally, you should look to have the long side of each bed facing south for maximum exposure to light. If you have the narrow end facing south, you may find that taller plants limit the amount of sunlight allowed for smaller plants at the back.

Plan out your garden, but remember to allow a generous amount of space between each bed to allow for paths. If you are planning on having grass between the beds, be sure to allow enough space to accommodate your lawnmower. Even if you are planning on paving the paths, you need to ensure that you have sufficient space to move a wheelbarrow between the beds. You can minimize the maintenance of the paths by using a membrane underneath the flagstones to reduce the risk of weeds.

You will also need to give some consideration to what material you will use for your raised beds. Most traditional types of raised bed are made from cedar. The reason for this is that the wood is naturally resistant to rot. However, there are other materials available for your raised beds, such as composite or recycled plastic, which may be more appropriate for your garden. You can also use other materials such as flags, which can be painted or decorated to complement your garden aesthetic.

You may also wish to consider adding a trellis to your raised beds. Most raised beds are sufficiently sturdy to support a trellis system. This allows for support for climbing flowers or vegetables such as beans. There are many types of trellis which can be attached to your bed without visible holes and the potential to relocate the trellis to other beds.

Before you begin planting or growing, you will need also to plan and prepare the garden. If the ground is new to gardening, you should double dig the area for the bed to at least a depth of sixteen inches. This will allow you to pull any stones and to check the soil composition. You can also check for any signs of roots in the bed area. This will show if you need a root barrier for living trees, such as a massive plastic sheet. If you pile the soil up in the center of the area, you will be able to set the new raised bed into place without needing further digging.

If you have had an issue with burrowing animals in your garden, you will also need to plan for this. Most burrowing pest problems can be overcome by using a half-inch layer of hardware cloth in the bottom of the raised bed before you add the soil. The mesh should overlap the edges of the raised bed to a height of at least three or four inches. Stapling in the cloth will prevent it from being disturbed.

When you are planning out the beds, be sure to check that they are completely level. Ensure the soil is spread out evenly and level. Once you have added the soil, avoid stepping in the bed. When you step into the bed, you will compact the soil and cause aeration to be reduced. You should also train your pets to stay out of the raised bed or plan to have the beds in an area not accessible by the pets.

When planning out your raised bed garden, you can allow your creativity to shine. The beds can be arranged in meticulous rows or into a geometric pattern. If you have an abundance of space, you can plan your raised beds into a real garden feature.

Making Your Own Compost

A lot of people try their hand on one old technique which turns garbage to gold, which is known as making compost. However, its making may be mysterious to specific people or just too complicated. This belief, however, is not valid. Provided that you follow the given directions, you can make compost that is fit for use in your raised bed garden.

The first step is deciding to build piles or even bins in your own yard. You can decide to use drums or even tumbler systems, which make compost quick in a space that is small. It also is possible for you to have worms or even larvae incorporated to consume the garbage you place inside and accelerate the composting process.

First, select a spot that is out of direct kind of sunlight and right out of the rain, yet still near raw materials or the garden or the place where this ought to be utilized. The second step is gathering materials. You can make use of vegetable scraps, grounds of coffee, tea leaves, fallen leaves, manure, and organic plant materials. However, do not use the manure of humans, cats, dogs, and caged birds. You also have to avoid weed seeds, diseased plants, meat, and oil.

You then have to shred or even chop materials which are substantial. Know that for materials of the raw kind to be broken in the process of composting, fungi, as well as bacteria, require access to plant surfaces of the most kind. Chop and even shred things, so these do not take long to decompose.

In building your pile, alternate the layer of materials that are brown in colour with the green ones. Another option that you have is mixing everything all together. If necessary, moisten it to make it damp and not too wet. If you happen to make use of piles of the traditional kind, you may decide on having the whole thing left as it is. Nature works quite slowly, breaking down what organic materials are placed in around eight months to a year.

If it happens that you make use of drum, grub, or the worm composters, you will not need to have ingredients layered. All that you need is throwing everything in it. Should you make use of a sphere or a drum system, make sure of rotating or even turning your tumbler, so it mixes well. When choosing worms, red wigglers have been known to be the best for processing compost.

Another step, despite being optional, is to have it screened. This allows you to get the more giant sticks and even stones right out of the product, which is already finished. One sign that your compost is already ready for use is when this is crumbly, rich, and dark. Also, it is ready when you can no longer see the raw materials in it.

The last step is using it in your raised bed garden for planting seeds, added to soil, and for top-dressing the plants that you have. Know that using this material for gardening allows for plants to be healthier and more beautiful.

Chapter 1
The Basics

Choosing Raised Bed Gardening

While a few people think the additional work of raised bed gardening isn't justified, despite any potential benefits, there are a few points of interest that you may wish to consider. First, for the individuals who don't have a clue what raised bed gardening is, we should characterize it. In most essential terms, it is the point at which a planting zone is an arrangement, and the soil is mounded a couple of creeps above level ground. This can get progressively unpredictable with rail street ties and different sorts of dividers to assemble a higher structure. The significant part is that the soil is over the ground level, and there is no lying water. A portion of the benefits of raised bed gardens include:

- The plants are simpler to access, and you don't need to twist down as far to get to them.

- Since the plants are close enough, and you can develop beyond what you can in ordinary lines.
- The soil has better drainage, so there is less sickness.
- The soil heats up quicker in the spring and doesn't cool as quick in the fall.
- You don't stroll on the soil, so it doesn't get compacted. Numerous individuals don't understand that roots need air, and in this manner, compacted soil is exceptionally adverse to plant development.
- Some feel that the garden is increasingly beautiful as it has a predetermined geometry and structure.
- Studies have demonstrated that a raised bed garden might be up to multiple times increasingly profitable per square foot contrasted with typical gardening procedures.

While you may make the raised bed garden to any shape, there are a few rules to follow. The garden can be any length that you need. However, it shouldn't be more than 4' wide so that you can arrive at it quickly from either side. It very well may be as high as you need it, yet remember that the higher you go the more help you should assemble. Indeed, even a 6 - inch raised bed will give you huge advantages. Raised bed gardens don't should be confined, yet by not encircling them, you hazard losing soil to disintegration. You should fill your raised bed garden with new soil, fertilizer, and all-around matured excrement.

An appropriately structured raised bed garden will be spread out with the goal that you never need to stroll on the soil. The dividing will permit you to walk along the lines, in this way, never contacting the ground. If you decide to outline your garden with wood, make a point not to utilize pressure treated timber. This has been known to drain synthetic compounds into the soil. While untreated wood won't keep going as long, it is a more secure other option. Another option is to utilize reused plastic/wood composite timber. The drawback to using this to outline a raised bed garden is the way that it costs up to 40 per cent more than standard wood.

There are a few instant units accessible that let you rapidly and handily set up a raised bed garden. A significant number of these units are made of red cedar wood that is usually impervious to spoil and creepy crawlies. Red cedar doesn't have any destructive synthetics that may filter out into the soil.

If you love to eat crisp, natural vegetables, then don't care for pulling weeds or adding to a significant water bill with a customary column garden. At that point, you're going to cherish square foot gardening. Square foot gardening is done in a 4 ft. raised garden bed, which comprises of four sideboards and no base. You should put down a weed boundary to make the base. At that point, you fill the bed with an uncommon soil blend: three equal pieces of vermiculite (to hold dampness), peat greenery (to make the soil light and free for drainage), and fertilizer (for supplements). You can discover these at your closest nursery or garden shop. In case you're on edge to begin on your raised bed garden immediately, simply purchase the business manure until further notice. In any case, it would be justified even despite your opportunity to begin making your natural manure for some other time. It's an incredible method to use the supplements in your kitchen vegetable pieces and grass clippings, just as get a good deal on business manure.

The most helpful approach to make your fertilizer is in an encased manure tumbler. At that point, you don't need to manage the unattractive wreckage, scent, and bugs of an open manure load. Search for a composter that is planned with a large, removable cover for simple access and a simple to-turn wrench. It takes several months to separate original pieces into rich manure for your plants, so you'll need to kick your custom - made fertilizer off ASAP.

Presently the way that you have your extraordinary soil blend contained inside the dividers of this raised bed implies you will appreciate quick and particular points of interest that you wouldn't get with customary line gardening. The soil right now will never be strolled upon or bowed upon, and along these lines won't become compacted. This implies a few preferences for you. Most importantly, no rototilling will be essential next season, and less watering will be required. The free soil will permit appropriate water drainage and dampness maintenance—another preferred position to having your plants contained in a 4 ft. square bed is the way that you can undoubtedly get to any zone of your garden from the side of the bed without entering the garden itself. Presently isn't that a progressively down to earth approach to spread out a garden?

Plant separating in square foot gardening is done on a network with each square foot containing another kind of plant. Before planting, it is astute to separate this network with twine to guarantee appropriate plant dividing. What number of plants you put in each square relies upon the size of the plant will be the point at which it has developed. For instance, it is prescribed to put just a single tomato plant for each square foot since it is a productive vine plant. Yet, you could put up to four strawberry plants in each square. Plants with sprinters that take up yards and yards of room, for example, squash and cucumbers, should be developed vertically on a robust casing. For profound established plants, for example, potatoes or carrots, you'll need an extra-profound bed with at any rate 12 creeps of soil.

You can assemble your own raised garden bed, or you can purchase a business unit. Business raised bed packs are advantageous because the boards have been pre-estimated, and they incorporate all the vital equipment. In case you're an apprentice, you'll need to search for one that accompanies a convenient how-to guide of accommodating counsel and tips. These business units are accessible with wooden or plastic sideboards.

Raised Garden Bed packs made with plastic boards offer a few points of interest over wooden garden beds. They won't twist, decay, or draw in creepy crawlies. Plastic boards are helpfully lightweight and smooth, and you don't need to look out for fragments. A plastic raised garden bed with an interlocking board configuration can be collected in under 60 minutes. Some of them accompany a clear vinyl "promising start" walled in area, which is particularly pleasant to have in regions with a short developing season. The beds in these raised garden units can be utilized independently or twofold stacked to make extra-profound beds. The interlocking structure likewise permits you to destroy the bed and migrate it fundamentally effortlessly.

So, get you a raised garden bed and a manure tumbler and check out square foot gardening. It's an inventive mid-year action from which you can receive loads of delectable benefits!

Raised Bed Gardening Ideas

Utilizing a raised bed garden is the ideal answer for zones with hard to work soil and poor drainage. There is a wide range of raised bed gardening thoughts accessible, include your imagination to make your garden individual and stand apart from all the others.

Raised gardens can come in numerous unique shapes, sizes, and numbers. You can decide to have one huge garden or a few little ones. Littler gardens appear to be a lot simpler to think about.

To add style to your garden territory, attempt shapes other than a customary rectangular one. Hexagons can add a lot more importance to the zone, and they are still simple to lie out and construct.

There are a few selections of materials to utilize. You can get raised bed gardening thoughts by strolling around your nearby garden habitats and home improvement stores. Pick something that will mix pleasantly with your home and the encompassing arranging.

Wood

Is a typical decision among raised bed gardeners? It is promptly accessible and straightforward to work with. Rail street ties make a rustic look, while planed blunder shows up increasingly wrapped up.

Weight treated timber

Will last longer than ordinary wood, yet it isn't the most secure decision if you will be developing vegetables in the garden. Redwood and Cedar are non-treated woods that last longer than different assortments, and they would be a superior decision for developing nourishment close.

Stone

Can make numerous sorts of raised bed gardening thoughts, it additionally keeps going any longer than any of the assortments of wood and can be found usually. It tends to be utilized with or without mortar, contingent upon the look you are attempting to accomplish.

Cement

Can be bought in beautifying shapes at the garden habitats, at sensible costs, this additionally can be utilized with or without mortar. If you like utilizing reused materials, you can accumulate broken bits of cement for an exceptionally special appearance.

Block

Is a brilliant decision for developing a raised bed garden. It gives an exceptionally formal and completed look to the whole region. It ensures longer than every single other decision, with little maintenance. The main setback is the measure of work required to place it in. Mortar is vital. It might be useful to have an expert introduce it.

Something else to consider with raised bed gardening thoughts is the thing that sort of plants to place in the garden. If its sole intention is to be ornamental, you may plan to utilize rich green foliage, blossoming plants, and bushes. Pick ones that do well in your atmosphere. Think about if the garden is in full sun, conceal, or a mix.

Vegetables are a famous plant to develop in raised beds. They genuinely advantage from the great soil and impeccable drainage. Most vegetables are appropriate for this kind of garden. Remember the measure of room you have when selecting which assortments to plant.

Why Raised Bed Gardening Is Easier

I believe that I am sold on raised bed gardening now. I was a little wary about it in the past because customarily, we dove in the soil and made the garden as it was done in the good old days. At that point, a year ago, we saw my neighbour were quite free with parting with additional vegetables. We happily took a couple because our garden was submerged and afterward under weeds. As summer wore on, the conventional garden turned into a waste. Along these lines, I currently have what a few people call a redneck garden. Yet, it's my variant of a raised bed garden, however better than a year ago's weed fix.

You would be keen on raised bed gardening if I said it makes gardening simpler from various perspectives? Sure, there was a little work placing the encircling in and purchasing the manure. However, it illuminated issues with the soil, controls bother, improves the measure of productivity in a zone, diminishes weeds, and they enable preserve to water .

Chapter 2 Advantage Of Gardening Raised Bed

There are a couple of authentic positive conditions of gardening in gardening raised beds. Some bit of the interest is to make an organized look to the nursery. Some segment of the central focuses is causing ideal conditions for plants so they too can be genuinely made sense of how to make critical returns in reasonably little zones. The most captivating part to me is that it makes developing more straightforward. Gardening raised beds in like manner offer the ability to create food or blooms in domains that would somehow are unacceptable.

- Bed Frames Support Trellises, Cold Frames, Covers and Irrigation
- Improves Soil Aeration

- Improves Soil Quality
- Prevents Soil from Compacting
- Increases Soil Depth
- Longer Growing Season
- Higher Crops

Smooth Access And Lesser Work In Gardening

Raised Bed

- Access for Physically Impaired
- Bunnies Can't Jump
- Reduces Maintenance
- Can Work in Garden without Getting Dirty

Ability To Garden On Unsuitable Sites

- Can Grow on unreasonably Steep Sites
- Can Grow where Concerned about Soil Contamination
- Can Grow on Sites without Soil

Saves Water

- Water simply the Beds, Not the Pathways
- Deep, Compost Soil Holds Moisture

Improves Conditions For Plants

There are wide scopes of environmental parts that choose how well plants grow; anyway we can have the best ramifications for plants by improving the earth and controlling moistness. The development of a gardening raised bed thus mulls over increasingly significant soils and for better leakage of wet soils. Soil air dissemination is improved as wet soils are exhausted.

In spring, the earth in a gardening raised bed will warm speedier than soil at or underground level, so the developing season is hardly more. In any case, considering the way that earth is increasingly significant and better drained doesn't normally improve soil quality or improve crops. For this, we need to make the accompanying step. My Grandfather used to state "don't plant a $5 plant in a 50 penny opening". What he inferred was the explanation consumes $5 on a plant and a while later just leave it in the ground with close to zero foundation for the plant's flourishing. Same is substantial with gardening raised bed gardening.

Since we produce gardening raised bed doesn't this way suggest that we will have a greater number of vegetables than we understand what do with. To genuinely improve the earth, we need to use the Double Dig Method (see Soil Preparation). That approach to tunnel down the significance of two scoops, or around two feet and mix peat greenery and also compost into the neighborhood soil.

This will make light and all around circled air through soils with heaps of trademark supplements. Extends Soil Depth - Deep rich soil that isn't compacted is to some degree achieved by building a packaging or divider to raise the earth over the ground level. This is furthermore practiced by tunneling down to improve the soil at any rate two feet down.

Channels Soil - As long as the gardening raised beds are not water tight, excess water will exhaust away, at any rate to the virus earth level. I'm sure you have heard the articulation "Plant when soil is valuable"; anyway I don't get its significance? This is about the condition of the earth and not about a date on the timetable. The soil is beginning to warm and isn't too much wet. It is not hard to turn over with a trowel or scoop and doesn't outline pack.

To test the earth, grab a lot of soil and press it. Despite that it breaks down, it's set up to work. If it stays together in a ball, it is unreasonably wet or conceivably you have a great deal of earth.

Sandy soil and soil with heaps of compost will reliably be set up to work before earth soils. Allowing the earth to exhaust in the spring grants the soil to be worked. Counting excrement, peat greenery or even sand to earth soils similarly makes the soil be worked.

NOTE: Depleting Soil is a twofold edged sharp edge. Notwithstanding that gardening raised bed helps dry the soil in the spring, it will moreover dry the earth all through the mid-year when you needn't waste time with it to be so dry. In airs that get a ton of deluge, this won't be a significant issue. Where I live, we get only 13-15 slithers of precipitation for every year, so it is an issue. I have to water everything regardless of that I have to create something besides sagebrush.

I like structure gardening raised beds two feet down, so soil can be kept significant and coursed air through without diving so far down into the ground, anyway it would take an over the top measure of water to keep the beds watered during July and August. So my gardening raised beds are taking everything into account, 12 crawls over the ground which is a not too bad equality for my air.

Improves Soil Quality - The earth is enhanced the grounds that the gardening raised bed makes vertical space to incorporate manure and other characteristic issue to the nursery soil. Breaking down can happen most quickly in soils that are both wet and circled air through.

Shields Soil from Compacting - Part of soil quality is keeping up the light, significant flowed air through soils. So walking around the gardening raised bed is a no. Holding beds to 4 foot or less will allow coming to any place in the bed without wandering into it. I have a couple of beds that are broader than 4 feet. I either have a walkway down the center (8x10 beds) or I place wandering stones or sheets so we never need to step direct onto the soil. Walking around compacted soil is unquestionably not a genuine arrangement because the earth is starting at now compacted.

If you walk around recently tunneled soil that is two feet deep with stacks of regular issue, your impression may sink 4 or 5 inches. If you wandered close to a plant that was developing in that soil, a 4 or 5 inch indention may cut off all the roots one side of that plant.

Longer Growing Season - Beds grant soil to be worked before in the season and the earth beginnings warming earlier in the gardening raised bed than the soil at ground level.

Increasingly noteworthy profits for record of better, further soil gives plants free, significant, all around exhausted, all around coursed air through soil. Higher harvests per square foot is in like manner although we can truly regulate small gardening raised beds. A farmer that plants a gather in a 500 segment of land field wrinkles it to disturb weeds and to make light coursed air through soil; anyway he wrinkles it with a 10 ton tractor which in like manner compacts the earth.

Right when the collect is developing, he can simply check a little case of the yield to check for moistness, authentic development, frightening little animals or status.

In small gardening raised beds, significant coursed air through soils is more straightforward to keep up. Pretty much every plant can be checked at any rate on seven days by week explanation behind sogginess, proper development, frightening little animals or availability. Any issues can be promptly spotted and redressed. The entire bed can without a lot of a stretch is watered or just two or three plants that need water. A lone disturbance can be squashed or a lone leaf with aphids can be dunked in frothy water before the invasion gets a chance to spread. Notwithstanding that you check that a pesticide ought to be used, you pick what sum is used and which plants need it.

Bed Frames Support Trellises, Cold edges, spreads and Irrigation. A wooden bed layout readies a foundation to join trellises, supports or covers over the gardening raised bed. I in like manner want to affix spill line inside the bed plots with staples.

- Trellis
- Tomato Supports
- Support Bird netting
- Support for Fabric or Plastic Sheeting
- Irrigation Drip Line

Smooth Access And Lesser Work In Gardening Raised Bed

Reduces Maintenance - The physical edge of the gardening raised bed thwarts weed and grass roots from creeping into the bed. The significant, free soil makes pulling weeds fundamental and doesn't typically require tunneling instruments. Regardless of that the beds are constrained, gardening, weeding and gathering should be conceivable close enough for the way. Pulling weeds from light, coursed air through soil isn't proportional to pulling weeds from compacted soil. In hard soil, chances are you ought to reveal the weed or you chance cutting off the plant, surrendering the root to grow again.

In light soil, the entire weed can fundamentally be pulled out of the ground. Since it's not an undertaking, you will find that you are pulling a few little weeds when you find them instead of making game plans to pull weeds or digger the lines for a couple of hours on your following long weekend. In all honesty, I don't have a digger.

Can Work in Garden without Getting Dirty - With most traditional gardens, when you go out to plant, weed or procure, you change articles of clothing, especially your shoes, and since you understand you will get chaotic. By and by don't misjudge me; you can get grimy when turning over the earth in gardening raised bed. Nevertheless, for the most part, you can stay outside the gardening raised bed to perform most gardening assignments without wandering onto the earth.

Remember; some part of the explanation behind the gardening raised bed is to shield you from stepping on the soil. If you should step into the bed, place a heap up or wandering stone, so you step in a comparative spot as a general rule. This will shield the soil from compacting longer. Access for Physically Impaired gardening raised beds can reduce stooping and turning and can be attempted to arrange the pleasant height for someone in a wheel seat or someone that uses a walker.

Hares Can't Jump - I expected to incorporate this one. I read an online discussion about gardening raised bed gardening. One individual, new to developing, didn't have a ton of progress the past season since rabbits kept eating her plants. Someone suggested they manufacture a gardening raised bed adequately high to put it a long way from the rabbits. They created a bed that appeared to associate with 2 feet over the ground level and declared the gardening raised bed handled all the issues achieved by bunnies, since "hares can't generally bob".

Rabbits can ricochet. I have seen them do it, so I call that unadulterated trash; anyway perhaps bunnies couldn't care less to ricochet up into a gardening raised bed where they can't see the appearance spot. I can't resist speculating that fencing or little walled in areas would be a more affordable response for stopping rabbits in a little nursery bed; anyway I don't have bunnies where I live now, so I can't test either method. I should get warning from some other person that has viably discarded rabbit issues with gardening raised beds instead of fencing.

Ability To Garden On Unsuitable Sites

Can Grow on Sites without Soil - In urban networks, gardening raised beds can be used on strong, dark top, staggeringly compacted domains or even housetop tops. Gardening raised beds can in like manner be determined to amazingly unpleasant or sandy zones that regardless would be hard to plant a nursery. Can Grow on Sites that are too much Steep -

Steep slopes are not sensible for customary line developing, yet gardening raised beds gathered like yards can make proper locales to plant.

Chapter 3
How to Plant

Picking your Seeds

It's time to look at seeds now. The best thing to do is to buy your seeds earlier in the year, even during the wintertime months. Especially if you're in the northern climates, you can get better deals on seeds usually then, and I would recommend getting stuff online a little bit early if you can. Seed packets have very good instructions and detailed descriptions written on them. This information tells what the seeds are going to grow into, what they're used for, how to plant them. Carefully follow this information, and you'll be in good shape.

Some gardening terms to keep in mind:

Before planting or going to the store to purchase seeds, here are some gardening terms you should keep in mind.

Annual plant	A plant that thrives for one season or year grow
Bagged good	Bagged, potting soil, soil, or mulch.
Bedding plant	Annual flowers—planted in flats.
Bulk materials	Piled soil, gravel mulch and potting soil, gravel
Drought-tolerant	Plants that don’t need much watering
Edibles	Fruits, herb, veggies.
Evergreens	Plants that have leaves year-round.

Groundcovers	Fast-growing short plants that can serve as a lawn grass
Hardy	Tough plants that thrive in winter.
Native plants	Plants native to your region
Perennials	Plants that return yearly.
Pottery	Statue, ceramic flowerpot, fountain.
Remedies	Organic pest control product.
Seasonal color	Annual or perennial flowers blooming in a particular season.
Shade plant	Shade-needing plant that cannot take harsh sunlight morning
Sun plants	Plants that require a minimum of six hours of sunlight.
Tropicals	Potted plants, like hibiscus, better suited for the tropics and need to be brought indoors during winter.

Reading a seed packet

As a gardener, knowing how to read a seed packet when you visit your local home improvement is essential. Although each seed packet has some variation in design, the packet tells you the right seeds to grow. A vegetable seed packet has more information concerning harvesting.

Here is how to read any seed packet:

Flower seed packet

Common name

Scientific name

Plant type

Note: Annual flowers last for one season or year, unlike perennials d.

Seed weight

Seeds are sold in weights.

Planting time

You can find information about when to plant the seed packet. Some packets highlight the optimum soil temperature for the seeds to germinate as well as zone maps that tell you the best month to plant outside.

Row spacing

This is the spacing you have left between seed rows.

Plant spacing

Distance between seeds on the same row

Planting depth

Depth of planted seeds.

Plant height

This is the average height of a matured plant. Understanding the plant height will let to plant in a way that each plant enjoys enough sunlight.

Vegetable seed packet

A vegetable seed packet has more details than a flower seed packet. A vegetable seed packet tells if the seed is of heirloom or hybrid variety. It also lists "days to maturity," indicating the number of days between seed planting and vegetable harvest. The seed packet also tells a plant's resistance or susceptibility to specific diseases.

1. Common name

2. Scientific name

3. Plant type

Hybrids seeds are crossed from two different parent plants.

Weight

Seeds are sold in weights. And this information comes with how much space the seeds can cover on your raised-garden bed.

“Packed for” date

The “packed for” date indicates when the seed packet would expire.

Light needs

Most vegetables need full sunlight, but you should follow what the pack says.

Seed packet top

Gives more details about the plant. Indeterminate tomatoes grow nonstop while determinate keep growing.

Days to germination

The number of days for the seed to sprout. Germination is stimulated in high temperatures.

Starting seeds inside

Hot-weather vegetables are best started indoors in cold regions. "Days to maturity" is the number of days between seed germination and harvest.

TMVSWV

This letter combination shows which disease the plant is resistant too. In our example, it says the plant is resistant to Tobacco Mosaic Virus and Spotted Wilt Virus.

Reading a plant tag

When buying a plant at your local home-improvement, learning to read the plant tag is another important skill. While the design on the tag might be slightly different, tags often display the following information.

Common name

The common varies from location to location, depending on history, language, or culture.

Scientific name

The scientific name is the botanical name of the plant. The name is often written in Latin and constant worldwide. The first name is called genus. The second is called species.

Plant type

Plants often fall into several categories: vines, vegetables, tropicals, trees, shrubs, perennials or annuals, groundcovers, and bulbs.

Light needs

Light requirements vary in different plants. Most need a minimum of six hours, while others thrive in shaded areas. Ensure the plant you are choosing fits your area's supply of sunlight.

Plant spacing between

Spacing information tells how you how much distance each plant needs from the next. Correct spacing is vital to prevent overcrowding.

Mature height

This measurement shows the mature height of your plant. For shrubs and trees, this could take many years to reach.

Water needs

Some plants need more moisture than others do. Some plants can survive drought while others are water demanding. And the fact is, plants of the same group often have the same groups.

Starting Indoor and Outdoor

Once you have your seeds, which plants you need to start indoors and which ones that you can directly sow in the ground. Now, this varies on where you live. In northern and colder climates, it is recommended you grow hot-weather crops, like peppers, tomatoes, and melons—any crop that the seed packet says the harvest is longer than 90 days—ensure you get those plants started inside.

Starting early in the northern climates is the key to getting a good harvest. However, if you're in the warmer climates down south, you don't have to worry too much about that. You can start a lot of your seeds right in the ground in March or April.

While some plants can be sown outside directly, it is best to start some indoors and grow for transplant. Mostly, early fall crops can be sown directly. Hot-weather or summer crops with long growing season should be sown indoors.

The seed packet will tell you the best time to start a particular seed. For the northern climate, you can start seeds between late March and late May. The plant needs the right amount of time to germinate and grow to appropriate transplant size.

Start Indoor	Start Outdoor
Watermelons	Squash/Zucchini
Tomatoes	Radishes
Swiss Chard	Potatoes
Pumpkins	Parsnips
Peppers	Peas

Lettuce	Onions
Eggplant	Okra
Cauliflower	Garlic
Cabbage	Corn
Brussels Sprouts	Carrots
Broccoli	Beets
	Sweet Potatoes

Sowing indoors

Put compost or seed starter mix in a clean growing container—peat pots or seedling flats. Ensure you poke holes in the bottom of the container to allow water drainage. Follow the recommended planting depth on the seed packet. Some seeds require submersion while some simply need a sprinkling of soil over them. Some seeds need to be soaked in water or wrapped in a damp paper towel. Finally, keep the containers in a warm, well-lit place at around 60 F.

Ensure you have read the seed packet

Understand that not all seeds will germinate

Use clean containers—peat pots and seedling flats—with good drainage.

Fill containers with starter mix and don't use your regular potting soil

Plant your seeds according to recommended planting depth.

Choosing large seeds in the packet.

Loosely cover containers with a plastic cover to prevent drying out. Poke holes in the plastic to allow ventilation

Carefully water seeds

Remove plastic covering as seedlings appear

Move your containers to a bright window.

As your seedlings grow more leaves, start making individual pots and them with compost and potting mix. Carefully move the seedlings to the new pots, keep watering, and keep them out of the direct sun for some days.

Taking the seeds outside

Before transplanting seedlings (at the recommended time in your seed packet) to your raised-bed garden, you have to harden them off by preparing them for the outdoors. This means gradually increasing your seedlings exposure to full sun on the last few days indoors. Put each seedling in your soil; ensure you set them with soil around the root. Ensure you continue to water.

Direct sowing outdoors

Using a trowel, dig a 2-inch deep row in the garden soil

Plants seeds directly on the row, according to depth and spacing on the seed package.

Some seeds should be sprinkled while some buried, depending on the recommendation of the seed packet.

Cover seed your seed some starter seed mix and garden bed soil.

Water—and keep watering every day.

Planting seedlings

You can start your seeds and make them into seedlings or buy seedlings from the seed store. You can grow your seedlings in biodegradable peat pots. When you want to transplant them, take off the base of the pots and put them in the holes. For plastic pots, remove them completely.

Except for tomato seedlings, it is also recommended you plant your seedlings at the same depth they are rooted in their pots. For tomato seedlings, pull off the bottom leaves of the seedling and carefully bend the stem. Ensure the de-leafed and curved parts of the stem are buried. Always water your seedlings and seeds, but don't let the water touch the leaves.

Spacing

You can choose to plant in blocks or furrows on your raised-bed gardens. How to space your seeds or seedling on the bed is often written on the packet. With correct spacing, your plants will grow well. For vining plants, like tomatoes, pole beans, and cucumbers that need a cage or a trellis. Ensure you make space for these structures while planting. Your seed packet should provide information about planting depth, planting instructions, and spacing requirements. Some will even give you how to start seed indoors, their germination period, and days to maturity.

You need water when planting seeds or seedlings, as you need to water immediately after planting. You should have a garden trowel, some stakes, and cages, depending on the crop you are planting.

Planting time of the day

For seedlings, the best time to plant is in the evening—which is the coolest time of the day. This helps the plant acclimatize better. However, for seeds, you can plant any time of the day.

Rows and blocks

You can plant seeds either in blocks or in rows on your bed, depending on your choice or the information on your seed packet.

Chapter 4
Strategy and Planning

Planning Your Garden & Building Structures

Before you go for your raised bed gardening project, you need to decide so you will know what you will need and be ready with all the things necessary to make your project a success. Hence, right at the beginning, you need to make a checklist of all that you need as well as all the steps you should take to get your gardening project established and running.

7 Factors That Make a Great Raised Bed Garden

There are many factors that you will need to take into consideration when you build a raised bed garden. Fortunately, all these factors are easy to deal with, and you can set up your garden in no time – even if you have next-to-no experience in gardening.

Sunlight

How much sunlight will your garden require? This is perhaps one of the most important questions you need to ask before you start with your plan for the raised bed garden. For vegetables, the basic amount of sun requirement is about 8 hours of sunlight. There will be varied sun requirements for flowers – check with a gardening specialist or your local garden supplier. For a good garden, you will need to ensure you get adequate sunlight.

How Big Will Your Garden Be?

With the raised garden bed, you can choose how much area you designate for your garden. This type of garden is especially useful when you are living in areas where open space for gardening is limited. The raised bed garden can be made completely mobile – build it waist high and on wheels so you can push it around wherever you prefer: indoors or outdoors. The best design to use for this situation is the square foot garden – where the plots are divided into 1 square foot plots and built just as large as it will allow you to reach its center without too much strain.

Is Fencing Required?

The raised bed garden might require fencing but not in the mode that you would use for a regular garden. This garden will require protection from birds – maybe – and gophers or other animals that might burrow into your garden from below.

For this purpose, you should lock the bottom of the raised bed garden with wire mesh – the type used for chicken coops. This will allow the soil to breathe, will not interfere with water drainage, and so on. The mesh will prevent anything from getting in from downside; for above the garden, you can use specially made covers to keep the birds away.

What Type of Soil Will You Require?

Check with your local gardening center to find out what type of soil you need for the plants you are planning on using. You will need to know what levels of fertility you will need to have for your soil to ensure that your garden starts on a good foot. Specifically, you will need to know include how much organic matter, how much mulch, etc. is required to get the earth ready for planting of a new crop.

What Type of Plants Should YOU Choose?

While some plants can adapt in different time zones and climate zones, most do not. Even those that do adapt do so with a price. The plants that thrive in other parts of the world will often mutate slightly to adapt to their new environment. Therefore, it is best to decide what plants you'd like to plant depending upon the climate zone in which you live and the type of plants that are native to where you live.

If you are a beginner, try consulting the local gardening shop for reference or check USDA.gov to find the nearest local cooperative extension services.

You must choose the right plants, or you will end very disappointed with the results.

You will also need to decide whether you are planning to grow vegetables – and if so, make a list of vegetables you would like to grow or you may decide you would like to grow a flower garden in which case you would need to plan what type of flowers, what colours, and what fragrances you would like to have.

Pay Attention to the Seasons

You will also need to pay attention to which plants are best for which season and what you enjoy most for each season. In case you cannot be bothered with seasonal plants, then decide type of evergreens you would prefer. For help in deciding what to plant, you can contact your local gardening store/ center and the local extension services at usda.gov.

If you prefer seasonal plants, you will need to make a seasonal plan, so you will know what and when you need to plant to have flowers/ vegetables throughout the year.

Ensure You Have Some Basic Tools at Hand

You will need some tools – though raised bed gardening requires the minimum – such as a soaking hose, garden fork, hoe, weed by hand, and a medium-sized basket for moving soil and mulch around.

Planning Your Garden

What to Consider

- Location
- Size
- Height
- Drainage

Don't think because you have limited space you can't build a raised bed. Having the luxury of space in your plot will give you more options as far as planning goes. Still, you can reap a high yield from a property with a small space so there is no need to think it won't work for you.

Even with a patio you can create raised garden beds that will not only be productive in their yield but also give beautiful definition to the area. You will have to make certain design decisions and planning is an integral part of your raised bed gardening success with this design but don't be daunted, as what you are creating is the optimum environment for your crops to grow in.

In essence that is your overall goal for having a raised bed, as a raised bed will increase your crop yield while reducing the work you need to do to get there. The location and planning at the beginning of the process will pay dividends at the end but is integral as the first step in getting there as even with bad, or no soil you can create an edible garden to be proud of.

Space permitting, you want your raised bed to be roughly three to four feet wide and seven to eight feet long. This will give you room to reach over the raised bed from the sides to tend your crops as you don't want to kneel or stand on any part of your growing area.

With a raised bed system getting the right height is also of vital importance, by creating a raised bed you are eliminating many of the usual complaints gardeners have, bending, kneeling and accidentally walking or stepping on the garden beds!

Getting the soil into the optimum condition is something I remember my grandparents facing on a monthly and yearly basis. I will go into soil properties in a later in-depth. Still, in short traditionally if you are faced with compacted or clay soil, for example, you could spend hours digging in and trying to perfect the soil to plant your vegetables. Seasonally you will have to continue this process! So by building a raised bed system, you are eliminating this hurdle right away as you can build your raised bed right on top of that troublesome soil and then make your soil - location permitting.

Many gardeners have found that growing crops in raised beds rather than traditional ground beds can yield twice the harvest. The main reason for this is that plants respond better in looser, rich soil giving room for the roots to grow easily and along with the fertile soil, the raised bed gives good drainage.

Having a raised bed also stops soil compaction to maintain soil aeration at its optimum that traditional ground beds tend to suffer from.

As planting crops in traditional ground beds will inevitably lead to the soil getting compacted just by you walking along and planting/weeding each month or season, affecting the soil structure.

This is why the size and height are so important when planning your raised bed as you want to be able to reach over easily to plant your crops without any contact with the soil, also the fact you are building the raised bed with nutrient-rich soil and using compost just for your crops to grow in is of huge benefit to their quality, and this is a soil mix you will create instead of trying to perfect or alter your existing soil.

When thinking about the location of your raised bed, it's worth noting you need six to eight hours of sunlight for optimum growing conditions, so have a look at potential areas taking particular notice of any walls, fences or tree canopy's that may inhibit your raised bed from getting sunlight. Of course, this will change season to season but planning for sufficient sunlight is your aim here as too little and you will have stunted growth, or worse, no growth.

While planning my raised bed area I found this simple exercise of huge benefit, as it saved lots of work and heartache over time.

Draw a rough plan of your garden and note where the sun hits over a day at say 8 am, 10 am, 12 pm, 2 pm, and 4 pm. This will give you a good idea of the area or areas to build your raised bed based upon a full six to eight hours of sunlight per day if you find you have reduced sunlight or you are in a part of the world where seasons affect sunlight exposure throughout the year, then this is even more imperative you get this right.

Don't be scared if you don't have the full 8 hours of sunlight per day, but try to aim for the maximum within your garden perimeter. Still, unfortunately, this may mean you need to reign in your enthusiasm and undertake research for a couple of days instead, the beauty of this is that if you discover you only get 2-4 hours of sunlight per day in the area you want to grow your crops you may have to change strategy however if that is all you have to work with i.e. built-up areas, high garden walls, etc., don't worry as there is still an awful amount of food or flowers you can grow.

Once you have selected the perfect area in your garden, grab a blank piece of paper, and with a pencil, draw your house and garden on it. With a compass (or smartphone app) find North and South, which are essential, as you want your garden south facing to provide maximum sun exposure. Dependent on how much lawn (if you have one) you want to keep, highlight this as a no-grow zone and then what's left allocate for your garden beds. This may be a little bit of a dynamic situation as it's still going to depend on how much sun gets to these areas so please take your time, once this is done, just circle the areas and you have got the start of your raised bed system.

Another design feature to think about is drainage of your raised bed as it is also an essential factor to the success of the yield, the simple fact of raising the bed will aid the drainage, preventing waterlogging and maintaining the nutrient-rich soil you have added, think of your raised bed as a huge plant pot that without drainage will create an anaerobic environment, this will be further accelerated in heavy rains, making it hard for your plants roots to breathe, this will mean that the roots can't get the oxygen they need and so start to rot and therefore won't grow and thrive.

Chapter 5
How to Build your Own Raised bed

Building a Raised Bed Gardening

The advantages of growing on raised beds are many; first of all, with this technique, it will be much easier to differentiate the soil according to the needs of the plant, compared to the traditional cultivation on the ground.

By opting for this type of cultivation it will also be much more convenient and quick to work the soil and carry out all maintenance operations, it will be possible to drastically reduce the problem of weeds and, by avoiding compacting the soil with foot traffic, it will also allow a better flow of air and water to the roots of the plants.

Another significant advantage is that by deciding to grow our vegetables, rather than aromatic herbs or flowering plants, using the raised bed technique, it will also be possible to do it on the balcony, on the terrace or perhaps in an area of the garden that was unused because it has no land with the right characteristics.

In essence, this cultivation technique consists of raising the land destined for the plants and delimiting the different crops through the creation of simple structures obtained by assembling wooden planks rather than bricks or stones of various kinds.

Gardening raised beds is a practice that was used long before colonial times. It has become increasingly popular among home gardeners because they can be installed in small inconvenient places of entry, it is a solution for gardening on land that can be installed almost anywhere in a limited period of time. They are also a perfect way to attach an appealing aspect to your yard and can bring other advantages as well as being a workplace than a dug garden.

The elevated beds are garden beds that are designed higher than the surrounding land. They are constructed no more extensive than four feet so that work in them is easy to reach. The length you want them to be can be any length. The distance is kept small, and there's no need to walk on the field to avoid compacting the soil.

The advantages of a raised bedside garden include easy access to the farm, better management of soil conditions and higher yields with less square footage. They are a right choice for construction in areas of poor soil like poor drainage or rocky areas.

This gardening method is much less difficult for disease and pest control. The soil structure will significantly benefit from the mulching and the accompanying planting and create a healthier plant that can defend itself against these problems. The addition of organic mulch will also improve the structure of the soil and feed the microorganisms living in the soil. These microorganisms are necessary to work the soil and add nutrients necessary for plants to thrive.

Raised garden beds are an excellent idea. Depending on the size of the gardens, you can complete most of the weekends, create and plant a raised bed garden to blend in with your yards' natural environment and attract wildlife, including birds and butterflies. .

How to Build a Raised Bed Gardening Step by Step

The 'contained lifted garden bed' is the most commonly lifted bed. For several vegetable and herbal gardens as well as flower gardens, it provides perfect growing conditions. Many fruits also do well in raised garden beds, including strawberries, grapes and raspberries.

Steps for a wooden upholstered bed as most elevated beds are made from wood.

Step One

Selecting a location is one of the most important decisions you make while building an elevated bed garden. Select a region that gets full sun, as most vegetables need full sun. If you want to plant vegetables that require partial sunlight, either build another bed in a different location or find a location that receives complete and partial sunlight. Also, make sure the area is flat, so water is secure, and all areas receive constant and equal amounts of water. If you want to make watering quickly, consider installing a quick-to-use drip irrigation system to keep your garden watered.

Step Two

Decide your garden size and shape. Make sure you can reach all of your gardens without going into bed. Try to keep the garden long and narrow, allowing you to access all your vegetables without actually entering the garden. That's nice because the soil won't get compressed from running over it. This will give you carrots growing as straight as an arrow. Note accessibility is important, and if you want to place your garden against a fence, tries to make it just 3 feet long so you don't have to walk into the garden. The depth of an elevated bed garden is up to you, but the deeper, the better, especially if you grow carrots or parsnips that need deeper soil. If you can, make your bed 12 inches tall!

Step Three

Your site's planning is very critical. Once you have your garden shape and scale, start building the bed. Grab the existing sod and loosen the soil below to a depth of eight to twelve inches. This gives your garden extra depth and good drainage. To move quickly, just cover the current sod and soil with newspaper or cardboard.

Step Four

Now it's time to build the bed. Using rot-resistant lumber like cedar or one of the newer composite woods to create your bed, depending on the size of the garden, 'two by six' pieces of wood will create the entire garden. Cut the pieces to the appropriate length; add them to a simple frame. There are several different ways to add the wood, but choose one that is simple for you and can hold well for years of use.

Step Five

After building the frame in a spot, make sure you level your bed from all directions. This is a necessary move because if your bed is not level, you will find that water flows of the garden and sits in another. If part of your frame is high, just remove any under it until you have a level frame.

Step Six

It's time to fill your garden with soil and compost after levelling. This will allow you to create a garden with great soil, ideal for growing vegetables. You can plant or sow seeds when they are full and raked.

Wooden Raised Bed

Let's start with the classics: a simple wooden raised bed. The most popular frames are made from 2 × 6, 2 × 8, or 2 × 12 boards or 4 × 4 timbers. Galvanized wood screws or nails are strong enough to hold together a frame made of 2 × 6s or 2 × 12s, but 6-inch-long galvanized spikes or timber screws are needed to connect 4 × 4s. Consider your space and the space you'll need to go around your bed or beds, before starting. There are many different ways to create a wooden raised bed but the guidelines below provide a simple outline of the basic construction methods, feel free to adapt it to your needs.

Step 1: Gather your materials and prepare the site by stripping off existing vegetation

Step 2: You'll need two 6-foot lengths for the long sides and two 3.75-foot (45-inch) lengths for the short sides. Measure the lengths with the tape measure, and use the saw to cut the boards.

Step 3: Set the boards into position. If you're using screws, first use the power drill to make pilot holes in the wood. Then screw or hammer two pieces together at the corner. Or, you can cut lengths of 2 × 2 or scrap lumber to serve as corner braces and drive nails or screws through the frame pieces directly into a brace.

Step 4: Fasten together the other two frame boards at the opposite corner. Next, check to see if the frame is squarely aligned. One way to do this is to measure the distance diagonally across the frame, and then measure across the other diagonal. If the two distances are equal, then the corners are square. When you're sure the frame is squared up, add fasteners at the two remaining corner joints as well.

Step 5: Use a spirit level to check that the frame is level, or simply get down on the ground and eyeball it for levelness. If there are high or low spots, add more soil or dig out soil as needed until the frame is level all around.

Step 6: Fill up the lower of the raised bed with soil. If you had to remove grass where the bed was to be constructed, this can be placed upside down in the bottom as it will gradually rot over the season.

Step 7: Top off the bed with a 50:50 mix of topsoil and garden compost or general purpose compost.

Waist High Raised Bed

A waist high raised bed is perfect for people with mobility issues, and also a great choice for urban gardeners. It may seem a bit daunting to build it, and you may be tempted to buy one or give up on the whole thing. But I promise you that with this step-by-step guide you'll be done in no time and it will be a rewarding experience. These instructions are meant for a 6.5 by 3.2 raised vegetable bed, but you can easily adapt it to your needs, should they differ from these measurements.

Step 1: Once you have selected the area for your raised bed, I recommend that you clear a rectangle to a size of 7 by 4 feet. This makes it easier for the construction stages.

Step 2: Next dig out the 6 post holes to a depth of 2 feet. Use a spade to dig square holes the width of your spade. Try to keep the holes as straight and square as you can as this will add to the strength of the final construction.

Step 3: Now put in your posts: the posts are 0, 32 x 0, 32 feet and are 5 feet long. It's important that when placing the posts that not only are they the same height as each other that they are vertically straight. Place 1 post per hole and then follows the instructions on the post Crete bag. Allow to set and then move on to the next step.

Step 4: Now the cross beams: they should be 0, 32 by 0, 15 feet and 3, 2 feet long. I would suggest that you buy them pre-drilled to avoid splitting, so depending on the exact screws you choose to use drill holes 0, 03 inches less than the width of the screws.

Step 5: Next screw these cross beams 1 foot from the base and 1, 6 feet from the top of each post.

Step 6: Next install the first set of wall rails. They should also be pre-drilled

Step 7: Now it's time to screw each of the floor beams to each of the cross beams remembering to pre-drill before screwing them down. And now, the floor of your raised bed is completed.

Step 8: Be sure to drill 20 diameter holes in the base around 3 on every other board.

Step 9: Repeat step 6 for the rest of the walls.

Step 10: Using a staple gun fit a liner to your bed we recommend 2 layers of good quality weed control matting however you may use plastic but make sure there are sufficient drainage holes.

Step 11: Using 0.9 by 2 inches timber screw a piece in each of the gaps between the posts.

Step 12: Fill your bed: You will need either 1 bulk bag of compost or topsoil approx. 1 tonne to fill your raised bed. Depending on what you intend plant, you can fill the bottom with grovel, sand, pieces of wood (that will slowly decompose over time and feed your raised bed with nutrients).

Chapter 6
Soil and Planting

Know your Soil

Basic soil testing packs can be purchased on the web or from most garden stores. They are extremely simple to utilize and will ask you to recognize which plants your soil or manure will suit. An example of soil or manure is stirred up in a testing arrangement, and the shading the fluid changes to is at that point checked on the shading outline. 1 is amazingly acidic, and 14 are neutral; a pH of 7 is unbiased. It is prudent to take a couple of tests from various area of the raised bed to ensure an exact reading is being taken.

Corrosive soil

Adding compost to the soil can bring down the pH with the goal that it is increasingly acidic. If your soil is on the neutral side and you need to grow corrosive adoring plants, this progression is vital, and, in most gardens, this is enough. Make your own acidic compost at home by including heaps of spoiled pine needles, woodchips, sawdust, decaying leaves, or even new espresso beans to the compost heap. It will, in the end, turn impartial once more, so it is worth verifying each year and garnish with increasingly acidic materials if necessary. There are additionally acidifying items that can be purchased from garden providers. Sulphur is the most regular item used to ferment the soil, Sulphur dust being faster to ferment the soil than Sulphur chips. It just ferments the soil once it has been separated by microorganisms, so results are not momentary. It can take a long time, and conditions are sufficiently acidic to suit the plants' necessities.

Alkaline soil

Including mushroom compost or hardwood debris to the manure can be a viable strategy for making progressively antacid conditions. Then again, there are items that can be purchased, for example, ground limestone, ordinarily called “garden lime,” which has the dynamic element of calcium carbonate.

Calcified kelp and ground chalk additionally create calcium carbonate. Dolomite lime is a ground limestone that gives magnesium carbonate and calcium carbonate. Planters frequently use it to lime soils that are deficient with regards to magnesium. Continuously adhere to the producer's guidelines if utilizing these items.

Do recall that watering with delicate or hard water can likewise influence the pH of the manure in your raised bed. The material used to build the beds could step by step have a draining impact on the soil as well. For instance, new pine or treated wood could make it acidic close to the edges of the bed.

Work with your soil

Recall that anything you add to the soil will influence the pH balance is just an impermanent arrangement, and the best counsel is to work with your soil sort as opposed to endeavouring to transform it—a considerably more efficient arrangement that will likewise have a lot littler organic effect. Fundamentally, changing a soil's pH for any time span is certifiably not an extremely simple activity, except if you import soil.

Those with small gardens know the significance of ripe soil; however, don't feel a passionate longing to become familiar with the details of pH proportions and N-P-K balance.

What's the Point of Planting?

Deciding what to plant in a Raised Bed Garden is much easier than you might think. If you plan it all carefully, you will be able to enjoy a beautiful green space, rich in vegetables, without having to spend hours and hours working on it.

If you are starting to grow for the first time, it is advisable to start small and then expand as you go along and only after you have learned and acquired the basics. The risk, in fact, is to plant many more plants than you really need for your family's needs, an aspect that makes your garden difficult to manage, both from the point of view of the care to devote and the quantity of the harvest.

The plants that generally offer abundant fruit are tomatoes, peppers and courgettes, because they continue to produce throughout the summer; on the contrary, vegetables such as carrots, radishes and maize produce only once and - in this case - it is probably necessary to provide for a higher number of plants. creating a vegetable garden and taking care of it is not that difficult, but if you decide to start today it is appropriate to go step by step, starting with plants that are simpler to manage, and then try your hand at more complex ones, which require more care and time. Among the most suitable plants for beginners we recommend arugula and “Soncino” (valerian), but also radishes and carrots, which - as we have seen - are plants that produce only once, however they are perfect to start experimenting with the world of the garden.

The rocket, for example, should be planted from mid-March onwards (after the period of frost and the great winter cold): after cleaning and tilling the soil carefully, sow the rocket in holes, about half a centimetre deep, and spaced - one from the other - about 10-12 centimetres apart. Water regularly every day, at the end of the day or early in the morning, and within 7-10 days you will see the first seedlings appear.

Before picking it, you will have to wait about 30-35 days and - when cutting it - remember not to cut everything, but to leave a few centimetres from the ground, so that it can grow again.

If, on the other hand, you have decided to grow valerian, you can sow it from the middle of August to the beginning of November, following the same scheme indicated above for the rocket: create furrows half a centimetre deep, about 10 centimetres apart and then sow, taking care to irrigate correctly, so that the soil is always damp.

After a few days, you will see the seedlings sprout, which you can harvest after about 15 days. Always remember to keep the soil clean, removing weeds.

And now let us come to carrots, quite easy to grow, healthy - because they are rich in vitamins - and always precious and useful in the kitchen for many different preparations. Carrots, like rocket and valerian, are also quite easy to grow and can withstand very different temperatures, which is why they grow very well everywhere. In places where the temperatures are lower, they are sown indicatively (much depends also on the microclimate of the area) between the months of March and June, while in places where the temperatures are higher, they are sown between February and May.

The soil must be cleaned and worked creating furrows about 25 centimetres deep and removing anything that may disturb the growth and development of the roots, such as stones, roots of other plants, wooden sticks, etc. This does not exist if you have prepared the soil in the way described above. Once you have prepared the soil, you must proceed with sowing:

insert the seeds in the grooves you have prepared, leaving a space of 25 cm between one and the other.

Pay attention to the cleanliness of the soil and you will be able to harvest your carrots about 4 months after sowing.

Regardless of the type of plants you decide to grow, always remember that taking care of and keeping your small garden clean and healthy also means obtaining a higher production; in short: a well-kept space of 5 X 5 meters is able to produce more than a 25X50 meters growing area, therefore considerably larger, but full of weeds or sick plants.

12 Simple Vegetables You Can Grow at Home

Once your garden is ready for planting, there are dozens of different vegetables, flowers, and other plants you can grow. Here is a brief overview of 12 different vegetables that are relatively simple for beginning gardeners to try (actually, there are more than 12 vegetables here, but I've grouped a few of them together). Beyond these 12, there are many, many more. You are welcome to grow anything else not on this list: broccoli, corn, celery, hot peppers, artichokes, Brussels sprouts, herbs, eggplants, and much more. But if you want to start with the easiest stuff, this provides a suitable introduction. For in-depth growing information on popular crops, please take a look at my other books on growing vegetables (each of which is hyperlinked here): tomatoes, peppers, and eggplants; potatoes; fall and winter vegetables (including broccoli, cabbage, kale, carrots, and more); beans and peas; and squash, pumpkins, and zucchini.

For each of the plants on this list, you will need to apply a balanced garden fertilizer to the soil. Look for a balanced organic fertilizer at your local nursery or garden center and follow application directions on the package as explained in Starting a New Garden. Water the plants well and keep an eye out for any pest or disease damage Basic planting and growing specifications for each type of vegetable are provided below. All of these plants prefer deep, loose, well-draining soil, so hopefully by following the directions in Volume 1 of this book, you will have a good home for these plants in your new garden.

When to Plant

When should you plant them in the garden? Each description below includes a temperature range for seed germination. But to be more precise about a planting date, you'll need to start by determining your last average frost date for your region. This is the date after which there is a good chance you can plant without experiencing temperatures that would kill a plant. You can find your last average frost date in spring

Early in the spring, even before the date of your last average frost, it is fairly safe to plant leafy greens (such as spinach, chard, and lettuce), root vegetables (such as carrots, beets, and radishes), potatoes, and anything in the cole family (broccoli, cauliflower, cabbage/collards/kale, kohlrabi, and Brussels sprouts). In addition, you can plant peas and onions. In fact, as soon as the soil can be worked (which may be much earlier than your last average frost date), you can try planting the onions, peas, spinach, lettuce, and cole crops. Follow with the other plants in this group a little closer to the last average frost date.

If a rare freeze comes along, you may lose some plants, but in most years these cold-tolerant plants can handle what early spring throws at them. Some gardeners who like to push the dates as early as possible enjoy playing Russian roulette with Jack Frost. One way to handle this is to plant one third of your seeds really early, one third about when they should be planted, and one third a week or two later for good measure. That way, you do not risk your whole crop, but you still benefit if there's an early start to spring. When I first started gardening, I tried this sort of thing, but then I noticed that even the later-planted vegetables eventually caught up with the ones planted earlier. Now I just watch the weather forecast and wait for a warm, sunny week. Until then, I'm in no hurry to get my plants or seeds in the ground.

The heat-loving summer vegetables will go in the ground later. Included in this group are some of the plants you might consider starting early indoors, such as tomatoes, peppers, basil, and cucumbers. Other late-starters include corn, squash/pumpkins, melons, eggplants, and beans. While most of these plants will survive when planted outdoors on the last average frost date, many regions are still too cold at this time for the plants to grow happily. For the plants in this group, it is better to wait until temperatures warm sufficiently to fall safely within the temperature range indicated in the descriptions of each vegetable below.

Chapter 7
Harvesting

After you have done all the hard work, now it's time to relish the vegetables of your labor. If you are looking to get the best flavor and premier nutritional values from your vegetables, you should pick them at just the ideal time. We will discuss some of the harvesting and storing techniques.

Knowing When to Harvest

Most of the vegetables are harvested when they are young and tender, which means that harvesting the plants, fruits, and roots before they reach their maximum size. For instance, beets and carrots turn woody (tough in texture) and insipid the longer they stay in the soil.

To keep some plants more productive, continuous harvesting is required. If you keep on harvesting vegetables like snap beans, lettuce, spinach, and broccoli, they will continue to produce pods, leaves, and shoots.

An easy rule for many of early crops is to begin harvesting when they are enough for a one meal serving; members of the cabbage family, spinach, scallions, Swiss chard, lettuce, and radishes come under this category. These vegetables love cool temperatures so they are picked up in spring.

Here are some popular examples of vegetables with their ideal harvesting time:

- Brussels sprouts are ideally harvested when sprouts attain 1-inch width.
- Cabbage should be harvested when heads become compact and firm.

- Carrots should be collected when tops are 1 inch wide.
- Cauliflower should be harvested while heads are still white but not ricey (the florets are splitting apart).
- Cucumbers for slicing should be picked when 6 inches long; but for picklers, harvest when at least 2 inches long.
- Eggplant should be reaped before color dulls and the flesh should bounce back when pressed lightly.
- Lettuce and other greens should be harvested while leaves are tender and soft.
- Onions should be gathered when necks are tight and scales are dry.
- Peppers should be reaped when fruits attain preferred size and color.
- Potatoes should be collected when vines die back.
- Tomatoes should be picked when they are homogenously colored.

Harvesting should be avoided at the following times:

Many fungal diseases escalate in moist conditions, so be cautious while working in wet conditions; as brushing your tools or legs against diseased plants can enhance the chances of transfer of diseased organisms to other plants down the row.

If you are looking for the freshest produce; that is rich in nutrient value and texture, try to reap early in the morning when vegetables are at their peak flavor and also the moisture content is at the highest value. After picking, the vegetables can be refrigerated so can be consumed later in the day.

In the case of root crops such as carrots and beets; that you intend to store in a cold storage room or root cellar, you should wait as long as you can to dig up root crops especially in fall. Root crops have the ability to withstand frosts. However, this should be kept in mind that harvesting root crops before the freezing of ground is considered ideal. If the soil is moist, they will be easiest to reap. It is unadvisable to wash crops that are intended to go to a storage room, instead just gently dust off any soil particles.

Putting Away Your Vegetables

Once you have reaped your crops, you are only left with two options. Either can be munched right away, or stored to utilize later. Different vegetables require specific storage conditions for the maintenance of their flavor and texture. These conditions are summarized below:

Cool and dry: Ideally, temperatures should range between 50 and 60 degrees Fahrenheit, with 60-percent relative humidity. These types of conditions can usually be found in a well-ventilated basement.

Cold and dry: Temperatures should be between 32 and 40 degrees, with 65-percent humidity. You can attain these conditions in most home refrigerators or in a cold basement or garage.

Cool and moist: Temperatures should be between 50 and 60 degrees with 90-percent humidity. You can store vegetables in a cool kitchen or basement in perforated plastic bags.

Cold and moist: Ideally, your storage area should be 32 to 40 degrees, with 95-percent humidity. You can create these conditions by placing your vegetables in perforated bags (vegetables in bags without ventilation are likely to damage quicker) and store them in a refrigerator.

You also can create cold and moist conditions in a root cellar. An unheated basement usually works well as a root cellar. However, nowadays, most homes have heaters or furnaces in the basement, which make the conditions too hot for storing vegetables. But if you don't have a heater, or if you can off a portion of your basement and keep temperatures just above freezing, you can store vegetables like root crops and even cabbage for long periods of time.

Make sure your vegetables are well ventilated in the root cellar; you can store onions, potatoes, and other root crops in mesh bags. Hunt for a humidity level that's as high as you can get. To increase humidity, spread moist wood shavings or sawdust on the floor but keep the vegetables elevated on wooden boxes.

If you want to store vegetables, make sure you harvest them at their peak ripeness. Also avoid bruising the produce, because bruises accelerate rotting. Store only the highest quality vegetables for long periods of time; vegetables that are damaged or scraped are likely to rot and spoil everything nearby.

Freezing, Drying, and Canning Veggies

You can preserve vegetables three different ways. These three techniques are freezing, drying, or canning. These methods will make your harvest last longer than if you stored your vegetables fresh. Here is the brief view of all the techniques:

Freezing: This is probably the easiest way to preserve vegetables. If you want, just mash up some tomatoes, put them in a container, and throws them in the freezer where they will last for months. Some vegetables like beans or peas can be directly put into a freezer as a whole. But usually, you have to blanch them first to preserve their color and texture.

Blanching is simply the process of dipping the vegetables in boiling water for a minute or two and then placing them in ice water to cool them off. Then you dry the vegetables with a towel and freeze them in labeled plastic freezer bags.

Drying: This technique can be pretty easy, but it must be done properly to prevent spoilage. Basically, you dehydrate the vegetables by laying them out in the sun to dry, by slow baking them in the oven, or by using a commercial dehydrator, which you can buy online. Spoilage is always a concern, so before drying your vegetables, you may need to get some additional information. You usually need to store dried vegetables in airtight containers; lidded jars work well. This is to prevent any air contamination due to microbes.

Canning: Canning is usually employed for long periods of time as it has the ability to keep the taste better in the middle of winter. But canning is a gentle and arduous procedure that can require peeling, sterilizing jars, cooking, boiling, and a lot of other chores.

Chapter 8
Planting Out Your Raised Bed

Planting Out Your Raised Bed

What to plant

When deciding what to plant in your raised bed, there are a number of things to take into consideration. These could include the following:

How many raised beds do you have to plant? More than one bed means that you can have a larger crop of one single vegetable kind.

How big is your family, or how many do you intend to feed?

Does your raised bed get full sun, i.e. at least 6-8 hours per day?

What do you like to eat? This may sound like a silly question; however it is easy to grow something just because you can. Only to find that it is wasted at the end of the season because you do not really like Brussels sprouts for instance!

Did you use this bed last year, and if you did, what did you grow on it? Good crop rotation is key to getting a great harvest.

As you may understand, what to plant is a question that has many answers depending on your individual wants and needs – as well as the wants and needs of your friends and neighbors!

For this reason I will cover a few different planting regimes that hopefully may give you some ideas of your own.

Crop Types

First of all we must divide the crops into their respective families, in order to get the best out of the soil conditions they are planted in.

Root Crops: Potatoes, carrots, parsnips, beetroot, fennel, celery

Brassicas: Cabbage, Brussels sprouts, cauliflower, broccoli, radish, swede turnip

Legumes: Peas, mange tout, French and broad beans

Alliums (onion family): Shallots, onions, garlic, chives, leeks

Solanaceae: Aubergine, potato, tomato, peppers, eggplant

Cucurbits: Cucumber, squash, pumpkin, melon, marrow

Miscellaneous: All fruits, lettuce, herbs, sweetcorn, chicory, asparagus

Though this is by no means an extensive list, it does give a good selection of the most commonly grown vegetables, and is more than enough to get started with!

Watch your height

One of the things that is easy to over-look, but most important, is to be aware of the height of the plants. Plant the high plants or climbers in the north end of the bed, that way they will not shade the rest of your crop from the all- important – life giving – sunlight.

In other words, if you have a raised bed that is broadside on to the sun for most of the day, then perhaps a frame built along the back of the bed would be a good idea. This would enable you to grow runner beans, peas or cucumber plants, making an excellent backdrop to the vegetables in the rest of the bed.

Peas would have the added advantage of adding nitrogen to the soil that would ensure a great harvest from the likes of cabbage or cauliflower that are particularly nitrogen hungry plants. It is also true however, that all plants like some nitrogen in their diet of nutrients, and so this technique would benefit just about everything.

A Single Crop

Planting a single crop in a raised bed – like the example in the first picture – is usually only done if you have more than one bed in which to grow your vegetables. After all what is the point in growing just one crop, unless of course you are a fanatical pumpkin grower, or just cannot see past a good cucumber harvest!

If however you do just have one crop in mind then that is fine. Your choice however should not just be on what you like, but rather on what you have grown in the bed– if at all.

Good crop rotation is not only important as to the nutrient value, but also for pest control and issues such as blight and fungal growth. If you have suffered a case of potato blight the year for instance, then you would not want to try and grow the same crop again this year as the potato blight virus can remain in the soil for several years.

Similarly it is not a good idea to grow onions in the same bed for more than two or three years running, if you want to get the most out of your harvest.

Raised bed using cages for plant support

Even with a single crop as your main crop however, you can still grow a 'companion' crop if you mix them correctly.

Companion crops are vegetables that get on well with other vegetables such as onions, carrots and lettuce or spinach onions and brassicas, being that their nutritional needs are similar, but their root systems collect the nutrients at different levels and so are not truly in direct competition with each other.

As well as giving you a variety of vegetables, this is a good idea for things such as pest control and less weeding as the veg blocks out the light to the weeds; and different crops attract different insects thereby helping control the spread of the insects themselves.

Antagonist crops are crops that do not do so well together such as Alliums (onions and garlic) with peas and bean crops. Crops such as beetroot get along with most plants and so can be planted quite successfully between onions or leeks without any problem.

Mixed Crop Examples

If you have just one raised bed and are trying out several varieties of vegetables to give you a good mixed crop, then some planting tips could include the following regime:

Tall plants to the back, on a fixed support of some kind where needed.

This could be planted with tomatoes, or peas, runner beans or cucumbers if the climate allows.

Sweet corn could also be used here and companioned with lettuce that will take advantage of the shade from the corn.

To the front of the raised bed could go any low-lying crop such as carrot, beetroot, parsnips etc.

If peppers are your main crop then you could grow spinach between the pepper plants. Again similar to the lettuce and corn example, the spinach will take advantage and flourish in the shade provided by the peppers.

If you stay in a cooler climate such as the UK, then you could try covering a portion of your raised bed with a frame similar to that pictured earlier, and cover with polythene. This will enable you to grow tomatoes and cucumber plants for instance, maybe even some sweet peppers – so expensive to buy in the supermarket!

To get the most out of a mixed crop the idea is about looking at the different vegetables needs regarding hours of sunlight and nutrient requirements. A good idea is to plant vegetables together that have different root systems, as mentioned earlier.

Planting deep rooted vegetables such as carrots or parsnips, means that you can companion them with shallow rooted vegetables such as beetroot, lettuce and arugula (rocket) to make for a good health selection.

Ultimate Mixed Crop

We can hardly discuss the idea of a mixed crop, without including a piece on the square foot example of growing mixed vegetables.

As mentioned, this is a system that is intensive farming gone to the extreme – but in a good way! The idea is that the old method of growing vegetables in a garden plot, where everything is planted in rows, is made redundant.

Instead we have a situation where a plot of ground – raised or otherwise – is set out in squares 1 foot square. Within these mini-plots a range of vegetables are planted, according to your needs and other deciding factors such as weather, nutrients etc.

The 'sales pitch' if you like, for this style of gardening include the following points:

A large percentage of a traditional vegetable plot is wasted owing to the fact that you must have pathways between the vegetables for weeding, harvesting etc.

With a proper rotational method of planting, you need never use fertilizer again, as the crops will feed themselves.

Far less waste than a traditional garden where all the cabbages, or cauliflower or whatever, is ready at more or less the same time, and has to be frozen, canned or given away.

Similar to a raised bed, the square foot method does not need such intensive care, due to the close proximity of the plants and the ease of gardening methods, particularly if it is used with conjunction with a raised bed garden.

One of the main strengths of this gardening method is the fact that it uses up very little space, especially if you go for the four foot square method. This means that despite this small space you can grow a complete range vegetables and have them all maturing at different times, depending of course on the length of the growing season.

That said, you have to keep a keen eye on any disease or insect infestation, potentially caused by the close proximity and there-fore poor air circulation, in this type of growing environment.

A square foot garden design lends itself very well to cultivating a full spectrum of herbs available. This in turn will ensure a garnish for every meal you prepare as well as some great tomato and basil salads for example.

Chapter 9
Paths for Raised Beds

Paths are an important factor to take into consideration when designing the raised beds. They can help to keep pests out of the beds and stop you trailing the garden into the house as the surface protects your boots from the soil. Leave a suitable gap in between the beds to allow for the path. Space the raised beds about 2'6" to 3' apart (75-90cm), making sure your wheelbarrow fits in the gap. A good test to see if the path is wide enough is to kneel down at the edge of a bed with your feet touching one bed and your knees touching the edge of the next bed. If you can kneel at right angles to the beds it means that you can work on the soil and vegetables without having to twist or struggle.

Suitable Path Materials Around The Raised Beds

Bark

Bark can be a pleasing topping for the paths. Lay on the paths to a depth of about 3" (8cm) it will last for the year. It is more effective laid out over a weed suppressing material. The resulting rotted material can either be composted or thrown straight onto the raised bed in autumn or early spring as a mulch

Bricks

These can be expensive but reclaimed ones will look great. They will be very long lasting and attractive as with the raised beds made out of bricks, check that they are totally frost hardy or they disintegrate quickly leaving sharp edges.

Concrete

Very permanent, unless you are totally convinced you will not change anything around this type of path isn't recommended. It is trouble free though and just needs a sweep every so often.

Grass

Grass is effective and will need regular cutting. Make sure the lawn mower can get between the beds. A strimmer will be needed to get up to the beds otherwise you will find couch grass will start so spread everywhere.

Gravel

Gravel can be very decorative and comes in a lot of different sizes and colours. It is an expensive option but last a long time and if it is laid over weed block will make weeding out perennial weeds a lot easier.

Landscaping fabric

The fabric is hard to keep down in windy conditions. The plastic woven material can be quite long lived and is ideal for polythene tunnel paths. The cloth material needs to be covered over with wood chip or gravel to be efficient.

Lawn chamomile

Not widely used but a beautifully fragrant surface that does not need mowing. It might not be able to cope with heavy traffic though if you have a busy plot.

Old carpets and rugs

Top quality wool ax minster on your paths could make you the envy of the neighbourhood. It is sometimes better to cut the carpet into strips slightly wider than the paths then tuck to overhang under the wood in the raised bed. Only use the best natural carpets for the job otherwise you will find yourself picking strands on nylon out of the ground for years as the top material rots and leaves the woven

Paving slabs

Slabs come in various colors and sizes to suit your garden style it is important these are laid properly to stop them becoming a tripping hazard. They can be enhanced by edging them with reclaimed bricks.

Plastic sheeting

This isn't perfect but thought it was worth a mention. Non porous plastic sheeting could cause puddles to form when the rain lands in it. The surface is slippery too which could cause materials such as woodchip or gravel to move unexpectedly, which could result in injury. If you do use this method, ensure it is well covered and put some drainage holes in the sheet with a fork.

Railway sleepers

These will look great along a path although they might get a bit slippery when wet. Be wary of the tar and creosote soaked ones though. Apart from the leeching of toxins, the tar will melt in really hot weather and stick to your shoes.

Sawdust or shavings

These will look good at first, but rot down quickly. Like woodchip this can be put on the beds after the year is out or add more material to the top to redo the surface.

Straw over thick newspaper

This looks good at first but will need renewing regularly. Fresh straw, like woodchip could initially starve your beds of nitrogen if thrown on the beds too early. Allow the old material to rot down well in the compost bin first.

Growing upwards

Making structures for climbing plants to grow up requires a bit of patience. The structures need to be able to withstand the pressure of the plants as well as any adverse weather conditions. Raised beds have the benefit of being able to use the edges as a prop for the poles.

Materials to use for the poles: Experiment with what you have locally. Bamboo, willow and hazel are all good. Tie strong knots and check regularly for any slippage or loosening.

Growing upwards in this manner with plants such as peas and beans means you can get a lot more produce from a smaller space which is ideal for ting gardens. It's also extremely handy to grow things against a wall.

Chapter 10 Maintaining Your Raised Bed Garden

Once you have seeded your raised bed garden and have raised the seedlings into young plants, you are still going to need to pay careful attention to your plants and their needs. As the gardener looking after these beds it is up to you to properly water and fertilize your plants. It is up to you to repair the frame and amend the soil. And it is up to you to watch out for pests and to prevent disease from entering into your garden. While you could skip these steps, your garden won't stay healthy unless you follow through with them all. You will need to get a feel for your garden and come up with a schedule that works for you but even more important is that it works for your plants.

But while all of these are necessary, they aren't difficult. In fact, raised bed gardens are easier to maintain than traditional gardens are and depending on the size of your beds you may not even have to bend down to work on them anymore. The height of a raised bed makes it easier to maintain and the contained environment means there is less that needs to be checked. But there is no such thing as a 100% maintenance-free garden.

Amending the Soil

As gardeners, our goal should be to keep our garden as healthy as can be so that it continues to produce fantastic results year after year. But doing this shouldn't mean spending a lot of money. A little bit of attention from time to time will allow you to keep the same soil in your raised garden bed for years without a problem. To look after our soil, we're going to amend it occasionally and make sure it is protected throughout the winter. By taking care of it before the start of winter and just after the end, you'll be able to keep your soil healthy for many seasons to come. You should still check on the quality of the soil when you can but this won't be necessary when the following steps are heeded.

When we mixed up our soil for our raised beds, we start from a base of 33% compost. This means that there are lots of nutrients in our garden soil to begin with. But as each harvest passes, there are going to be fewer and fewer nutrients in the soil. You should add compost either after you finish harvesting or in early spring when you start to prepare the beds. You will only need to do this once a year, otherwise you could overload your soil. While this is one way to get lots of nutrients into the soil, we'll also be using a liquid fertilizer in a few moments and this will ensure that there are tons of nutrients available to the plants.

But it is important to realize that there is such a thing as too many nutrients. When you or I eat, we stop after we get full. Plants can't do this. If there are too many nutrients in the soil then they may suffer nutrient burn. The edges of leaves will gradually curl up like the legs of a dead spider and it'll start to change colors. It's an ugly sight. If you start to see signs of nutrient burn then you should slow down and use less fertilizer. You may need to check the pH level of the garden bed to make sure it is still within the proper levels that it was supposed to be. If there are too many nutrients then you will want to water as normal but skip a fertilizer application or two so that the soil is flushed out a bit first.

The organic elements in the soil will break down over time. When this happens, they start to stick together much tighter and the pathways through the soil start to get blocked up. This makes the soil tougher for roots to push through while also blocking access to oxygen and slowing down the drainage speed. As you water your garden throughout the first year, be mindful of how long it takes to dry out and the way the water soaks into it. When you first start, it will seem a little odd to be watching the water this closely but over time it will tell you about the quality of the soil. When it starts to slow down and really change, typically after two years or more, then you will know what is happening. At the beginning of the new growing season, you can either amend the soil by adding more sandy minerals to it or you can replace the soil with a fresh batch. It can be expensive to replace the soil every few years constantly. Amending is the much cheaper way to go but you need to be careful and take it slow. You could completely wreck the soil if you added too much of one thing in without mixing it around and getting a feeling for the texture.

Winter is a big change in the weather and you need to prepare your raised garden beds to weather the storms. First off, most gardeners yank their plants out at the end of the season so that they can replant in the following spring. This is a good idea but you should only cut away the above-soil part of the plant. Remove any root vegetables as well but you want to leave the roots. Over the course of the winter they will turn into nutritious compost for your next crop. Speaking of compost, if you decide to add compost to the bed at the end of the growing season then you should make a layer of it on top, then cover this with a layer of mulch. This will make it so weeds can't get in, plus it will allow the compost to amend the soil and replenish many of the nutrients that were spent that summer.

If you aren't going to be mulching your raised garden beds then you should consider covering them using a strong plastic tarp. This will protect the soil and act in the place of mulch. It won't look quite as nice but if you are in an area where it snows a lot then you know that everything looks the same when it's buried in white fluff. It will be cheaper and far faster to put a tarp over your raised garden bed but mulching is the way to go if you are going to add compost before the winter. If you mulch, you can still use the tarp but it is rather redundant to use both methods.

By following these simple steps you can keep your soil lasting years. Checking on it throughout the season is important but making sure you prepare it for the winter and then "wake it up" again in the spring, it'll last you quite a while. The health of your soil is an investment well worth making. If you ignore it, you will find that it gets harder and harder to grow anything in your raised beds. You might think there is a problem with the bed while it is the soil at fault.

Fertilizing Your Raised Bed Garden

When you start seedlings indoors, you begin to fertilize them. When seedlings start to sprout outdoors, you fertilize them. As your plants grow and mature, you fertilize them. It is only just before you harvest any edible vegetables that you stop fertilizing them because you don't want to add any more liquid to the soil. Fertilizing your plants is an absolute must if you want beautiful flowers or large yields.

Fertilizer comes in two types. There are fertilizers such as manure which can be added to and then mixed throughout the soil. A fertilizer like this is a good application at the start of spring or end of fall. However, we can also mix in compost as a top layer with a blanket of mulch to protect our beds over the winter and add nutrients back into the soil. So we're not going to worry about fertilizers that mix into the soil. Instead, we're going to stick with liquid fertilizer.

There are many options when it comes to liquid fertilizers. Some gardeners brew what is called manure tea, which sounds as tasty as it smells. Another form of fertilizer is created by crushing comfrey until it oozes a sap which you distill in water and then feed your plants. For our purposes we will be sticking to the store bought liquid fertilizers but even here we have two options. The first option is to buy a premixed fertilizer. These are ones with the NPK ratio listed on them in numeric form like 30-30-30. If you get confused by the numbers on fertilizer bottles then don't worry, we'll cover that in a moment.

But if you do get confused by them then we're better off buying a premixed fertilizer rather than purchasing the raw materials to make our own. Whatever we purchase will still be diluted in water but the package can be read and it will have instructions for you to follow.

We've already referred to these numbers as the NPK ratio, so let's dig into what that means. Plants need a bunch of nutrients and micronutrients. The macronutrients they need are nitrogen, phosphorus, potassium, calcium, magnesium, and sulfur. Also included in these are hydrogen, oxygen, and carbon. Micronutrients for them include iron, manganese, copper, zinc, boron, and molybdenum. If you are adding compost to your soil and keeping it healthy then you are going to have most of these nutrients in place in the soil. This is refreshing since trying to balance all of these would be a lot of effort. We have to worry about six primarily. Hydrogen is found in water and we provide plenty of water to our plants throughout the growing season. We make sure that the soil drains quickly and this also lets both oxygen and carbon get to the roots and so half of the necessary nutrients are provided simply by paying attention to the soil and watering your plants.

The other three important nutrients for us to worry about are nitrogen (N), phosphorus (P), and potassium (K). Together, these three nutrients play the biggest role in the development of your plant. Nitrogen is used to make the leaves of the plant grow faster and come in more fully. Phosphorus is used by the plants to strengthen the roots and make them grow big and strong. Potassium is a general nutrient which is used in multiple functions of the plant that are required for it to properly use and distribute energy from the sun and the soil. The three numbers on the soil refer to these three elements. This is the NPK ratio or the NPK balance and it tells you the percentage of nitrogen, phosphorus, and potassium in the fertilizer. It will always be in that order, NPK, so many labels don't bother labeling the numbers on the front.

Knowing what these numbers mean makes it easy to understand these fertilizers. For most plants, select a fertilizer that is balanced around 30-30-30. This will provide a spread of nutrients to the plants. However, there are some vegetables that like a lot of one particular nutrient. For example, onions really like having lots of nitrogen and so you may go with a nitrogen heavy mixture with a ratio around 50-20-20. If you research your plants prior to seeding your gardens then you can group together those with specific macronutrient needs and feed them a separate fertilizer. If you are going with a general fertilizer then you should stick with the 30-30-30.

Conclusion

Thank you for making it to the end. There is something very special about getting your hands in the dirt for the purpose of creating or growing something beautiful. Home gardening has a way of letting people get in touch with the elements of nature and feel that they are a part of this amazingly beautiful world. This is one of the reasons why many individuals see the need to have some plants indoors or outdoors.

Some people consider gardening as a hobby while others do it for the purpose of having a supply of fresh fruits and vegetables at home. There are also those who want to embellish the appearance of their home outdoors with great-smelling and beautiful-looking plants. People have different reasons in having a garden at home, but they all reap the wonderful benefits of having it.

There are can many challenges in planting your own fruits, vegetables, herbs, and other plants right at your own backyard. Growing a variety of plants can require an arduous process, and you just need to learn the best ways to grow a productive and healthy garden.

Several varieties of herbs are easy to grow especially when you have already learned how to satisfy their growing needs properly. You can use herbs for medicinal or cooking purpose. In raised bed gardening, you do not have to hire a professional just to help you set up everything. There are many techniques available that you can use to build a fantastic raised bed garden. You can easily follow any of these methods, and choose which one can work best for you.

Starting to build a garden at home can offer you a great experience outdoors and help you learn some things. You can save your time, money, and effort by just learning about the pertinent information and techniques in gardening. You will eventually reap the benefits in having a garden at home just as long as you try your best to satisfy the growing needs of the plant you grow. Even if you are just a beginner, you do not have to fret as building an herb garden or raised bed garden can be both enjoyable and easy.

Make a great start now and enjoy the experience of having your own herb garden!

I'm a large fan of raised bed gardening for several of the rationale coated in this and other books. It's tricky to locate a drawback to this sort of gardening, so unless maybe you wish to incorporate the job and cost of preparing a bed that is raised in the first location. Yet even with this said, gardening will cost a few bucks to install. Nothing in this life is absolutely free, and whatever you dedicate yourself to perform typically has a price in time, substance or just plain psychological thought!

The bottom line however is that gardening, if in an elevated bed position, or only a conventional backyard situation; includes a lot of things to praise it. From increasing flowers to decorate your own life and the life of the others, to increasing veggies to feed your loved ones and possibly the remainder of the area, gardening is very good for the spirit and the gut! Many schemes are set up today to promote raised bed gardening particularly, as a means to bring entire communities together. Growing and sharing at the job of your hands has a true long-lasting value in any area, and is a good means of getting to know your neighbors. Kids particularly seem to get a true inclination to working at the backyard, particularly in the event that you teach them in a young age -- until the adolescent spots start!

CPSIA information can be obtained
at www.ICGtesting.com
Printed in the USA
LVHW042022291020
670161LV00001B/170